WITHDRAWN

DAY of the DEAD

Crabtree Publishing Company

www.crabtreebooks.com

Crabtree Publishing Company
www.crabtreebooks.com

Author: Carrie Gleason
Coordinating editor: Chester Fisher
Series editor: Susan Labella
Project manager: Kavita Lad (Q2AMEDIA)
Art direction: Dibakar Acharjee (Q2AMEDIA)
Cover design: Ranjan Singh (Q2AMEDIA)
Design: Ruchi Sharma (Q2AMEDIA)
Photo research: Sakshi Saluja (Q2AMEDIA)
Editor: Kelley MacAulay
Copy editor: Adrianna Morganelli
Proofreader: Crystal Sikkens
Project coordinator: Robert Walker
Production coordinator: Katherine Kantor
Font management: Mike Golka
Prepress technicians: Samara Parent, Ken Wright

Photographs:
Cover: Jose Gil/Maksim Samasiuk/Shutterstock;
Title page: Bobby Deal/RealDealPhoto/
Shutterstock; P4: Rdviola/Dreamstime; P5: Livia
Corona/Getty Images; P6: Felicia Montoya/
Istockphoto; P7: Lightworks Media/Alamy;
P8: Bluliq/Shutterstock; P9: Gordon Galbraith/
Shutterstock; P10: IDesign/Shutterstock; P11:
Cornishman/Dreamstime; P12: Joseasreyes/
Dreamstime; P13: The Print Collector/Alamy;
P14-15: Juergen Ritterbach/Vario Images
GmbH & Co.KG/Alamy; P16: Kim Karpeles/
Alamy; P17: Tony Anderson/Getty Images;
P18: Christopher S. Howeth/Shutterstock;
P19: Kim Karpeles/Alamy; P20: Mafaldita/
Istockphoto; P21: Cobie Martin/Alamy;
P22: Krechet/Shutterstock; P23: Omar Torres/
AFP/Getty Images; P25: Jaime Puebla/
Associated Press; P26: Jose Luis Magana/
Associated Press; P27: Russell Gordon/
Danita Delimont/Alamy; P28: David
Maung/Associated Press; P29: Livia Corona/
Getty Images; P31: Jose Gil/Shutterstock

Library and Archives Canada Cataloguing in Publication

Gleason, Carrie, 1973-
     Day of the Dead / Carrie Gleason.

(Celebrations in my world)
Includes index.
ISBN 978-0-7787-4279-1 (bound).--ISBN 978-0-7787-4297-5 (pbk.)

     1. All Souls' Day--Juvenile literature. 2. Mexico--Social life and
customs--Juvenile literature. I. Title. II. Series.

GT4995.A4G52 2008   j394.264   C2008-903116-4

Library of Congress Cataloging-in-Publication Data

Gleason, Carrie, 1973-
     Day of the Dead / Carrie Gleason.
          p. cm. -- (Celebrations in my world)
     Includes index.
     ISBN-13: 978-0-7787-4297-5 (pbk. : alk. paper)
     ISBN-10: 0-7787-4297-0 (pbk. : alk. paper)
     ISBN-13: 978-0-7787-4279-1 (reinforced library binding : alk. paper)
     ISBN-10: 0-7787-4279-2 (reinforced library binding : alk. paper)
     1. All Souls' Day--Juvenile literature. 2. Mexico--Social life and customs--
Juvenile literature. I. Title. II. Series.

GT4995.A4G54 2009
394.266--dc22

2008021204

Crabtree Publishing Company
www.crabtreebooks.com   1-800-387-7650

Published in Canada
Crabtree Publishing
616 Welland Ave.
St. Catharines, ON
L2M 5V6

Published in the United States
Crabtree Publishing
PMB16A
350 Fifth Ave., Suite 3308
New York, NY 10118

Published in the United Kingdom
Crabtree Publishing
White Cross Mills
High Town, Lancaster
LA1 4XS

Published in Australia
Crabtree Publishing
386 Mt. Alexander Rd.
Ascot Vale (Melbourne)
VIC 3032

Contents

Day of the Dead

Every October, children in Mexico plan for a special celebration. The celebration includes skeletons and yummy candy treats. The children are not celebrating Halloween, however. They are getting ready for Day of the Dead!

Day of the Dead is a celebration that takes place each year on November 1 and 2. At this celebration, Mexicans honor loved ones who died in the last year, as well as their **ancestors** who died long ago. They even make trips to the graveyard! Day of the Dead is not a scary time, however. It is a time for family, friends, and feasting.

● Children collect toy skeletons for Day of the Dead. In the Spanish language, Day of the Dead is *Dia de los Muertos*.

4

A Mexican woman dressed in traditional costume has her face painted for Day of the Dead. Day of the Dead is a celebration for people of all ages!

Smiling Skeletons

Skeletons are seen everywhere during Day of the Dead. The skeletons are called *calacas*. Children love seeing skeleton figures that are dancing or playing. People often decorate their homes with skeleton drawings and papier-mâché skeletons.

Teenagers sometimes dress up like skeletons and wear skull masks on Day of the Dead! They parade through the streets in their costumes and receive coins and treats from people passing by.

● This is a *La Catrina* figure. *La Catrina* is a **symbol** of Day of the Dead.

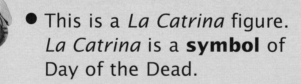

DID YOU KNOW?

Mexican artist José Guadalupe Posada created drawings of funny skeletons. His most famous work was called La Catrina.

Collectable skeletons, or *calacas*, line a street vendor's table.

Skeletons are an important symbol of Day of the Dead. When people see the skeletons, they are reminded of the beliefs of their ancestors and loved ones who have passed away.

Aztec Mexico

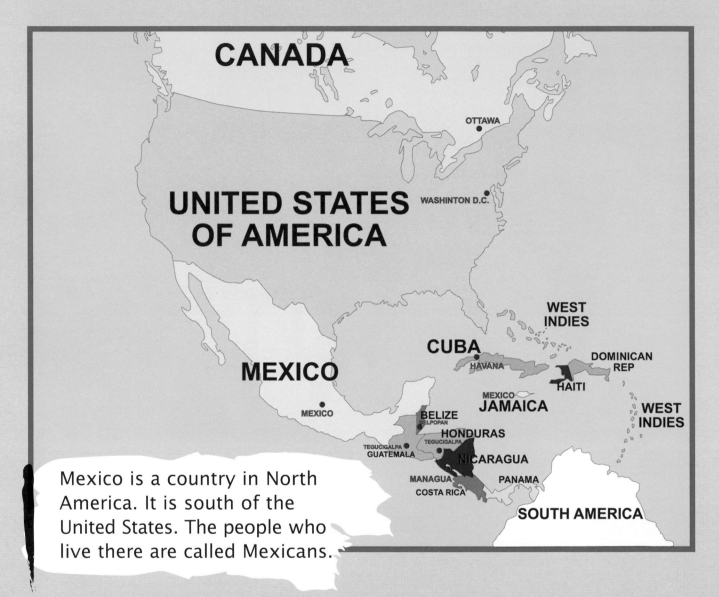

Mexico is a country in North America. It is south of the United States. The people who live there are called Mexicans.

The Day of the Dead celebration is based on Native Mexican beliefs. Long ago, many different groups of Native peoples lived in Mexico. Then about 500 years ago, Spanish explorers crossed the ocean and arrived in Mexico.

When the Spanish explorers arrived in Mexico, the Aztec were the most powerful group of Native people. The Aztec had built a large **empire** and ruled over many people. The Spanish took over the land of the Aztec and other Native Mexicans and ruled the country.

The statue of an Aztec god was built into a pyramid. The Aztec believed in many gods.

Warriors were believed to return to Earth after death as birds or hummingbirds.

During the Day of the Dead, Mexican people celebrate and remember the beliefs of their ancestors. Native Mexicans believed in many gods. They thought that the spirits of the dead could act as messengers between themselves and the gods. The Aztec believed death was another stage in a longer life.

The Aztecs believed that when people died, their spirits went on to an **afterlife**. In the afterlife, the spirits spent four years traveling through the **underworld**.

The underworld had nine levels through which the spirits traveled. The levels included fighting fierce jaguars and overcoming icy winds. The dead were buried with food, tools, and weapons they needed to help them on these quests.

The spirits of babies and young children who died did not go on the journey. Their spirits went to a place called Cichihuacuauhco. In Cichihuacuauhco, the spirits drank milk from the branches of a tree.

● One whole month of the Aztec calendar (shown here) was devoted to honoring the dead. During this time, the Aztec held many celebrations.

Honoring the Dead

The Spanish who invaded Mexico in the 1500s were Christian. Christians believe in one God and the teachings of his son Jesus Christ. The Spanish introduced the Christian beliefs and celebrations to Native Mexicans. Two of these celebrations were holy days called All Saints' Day and All Souls' Day. These holy days were held on November 1 and November 2.

● Crosses are a symbol of Christianity.

DID YOU KNOW?

All Saints' Day honors the saints of the **Roman Catholic Church.** Saints are Christian holy people who have died. All Souls' Day is a time to pray for the souls of all dead Christians.

Most Mexicans are **descendants** of Native Mexicans and the Spanish who took over Mexico.

In time, these holy days blended with the Native Mexican celebrations of the dead. The result of this became Day of the Dead. Although most Mexicans now speak Spanish and follow the Christian religion, they keep part of their heritage alive by celebrating Day of the Dead.

Some Day of the Dead symbols and practices come from Christian beliefs, while others date back to Aztec times. Crosses, for example, are a Christian symbol. The Aztecs sometimes displayed skulls to stand for death and rebirth. Day of the Dead skeletons are an Aztec symbol. The Aztec god of death was Michtlantecuhtli. He was depicted as a skeleton with a smile.

Today, Mexicans who celebrate Day of the Dead believe that the spirits of the dead return to Earth for one day every year. And every October, living relatives are busy preparing to welcome the spirits home!

The Aztec god of the dead was called Michtlantecuhtli.

Getting Ready

Young girls shop together at a market stall for Day of the Dead items.

The days leading up to Day of the Dead are a busy and exciting time. People buy what they need for the celebration. In some parts of Mexico, people save money for a whole year so they can purchase what they need.

● Accordions are played as part of Mexico's **folk music**.

Markets throughout Mexico fill with freshly cut flowers, baked goods, sweets, candles, toys, and decorations for the celebrations. In the cities' main squares, called *plazas*, vendors set up stalls or booths where people can also buy skeleton-shaped toys and jewelry. Folk music and dancing entertain people while they shop.

Mexican cut-paper decorations called *papel picado* often brighten up Day of the Dead celebrations.

Altars and Offerings

One of the most important preparations for Day of the Dead is setting up the *ofrenda*. The *ofrenda*, or altar, is an offering to the dead. At home, the whole family gathers together to set up an *ofrenda* in a corner of the room. The *ofrenda* can be placed on a table or on boxes covered in an embroidered white tablecloth.

● Cempasuchil flowers are called "Flowers of the Dead." The strong smell of these marigolds is said to lure the dead home.

The altars vary from home to home. No two are the same. Most *ofrendas* include some or all of the items shown here.

● Sweets are set out on the altar. Some candy skulls have the name of the **deceased** written across the forehead.

Families place many special items on an *ofrenda* to attract their loved ones' spirits back to their home. Copal is incense that is burned during Day of the Dead. Its sweet smell is believed to attract the spirits of the dead and to keep evil spirits away. Candles on the altar light the way home for returning spirits.

People believe that the spirits will rejoin their families for feasts during Day of the Dead. Families set out favorite food dishes, fruit, and water on the altar for the spirits. Photographs of the deceased, toys, and other personal items are also added. These items help families to remember those who have died.

INRI

Crosses and pictures of saints are placed on the altar with hopes that a favorite saint will watch over the deceased in the afterlife.

Food for the Feast

Food is an important part of Day of the Dead celebrations. Homes fill with the smell of chocolate, chilies, and spices as foods are prepared for the feast.

In the days leading up to the celebrations, bakers' shops fill with special Day of the Dead treats. *Pan de los Muertos* is a sweet bread that is flavored with orange and anise. It is also called "bread for the dead."

- Chocolate is a favorite Day of the Dead treat. Chocolate is made from the pods of the cacao tree, which grows in Mexico.

Pan de los Muertos is baked in many different shapes. Sometimes pieces of dough are baked on top that look like bones or other decorations.

Everyone enjoys eating *tamales* and *mole* during Day of the Dead. *Tamales* are corn dough filled with meat, cheese, and spices. They are wrapped in corn husks and steamed. *Mole* is a spicy sauce that is made from chilies, tomatoes, spices, chocolate, and nuts and is served over chicken or turkey.

Little Angels

Early on the morning of November 1, people honor the souls of children who have died. On this day, they believe that children's spirits return to Earth. Church bells ring to call the spirits, and the living, to the graveyard. The bells ring all day and night.

At the graves of children, families welcome back the children's spirits. The spirits are called *los angelitos*, or "little angels." Families put breakfast, toys, chocolate, flowers, and balloons on the graves. They even place a sugar skull on the grave with the child's name on it.

At noon, the spirits of the dead children are believed to **depart**. Families then prepare to welcome back the spirits of adults who have died.

With scrub brushes, buckets, and rakes, families clean the graves of their loved ones. Then, they decorate and set up an altar on the graves, similar to the *ofrenda* they built at home. Special candles that burn for a long time are set out. People spend the entire evening in the graveyard with the dead. It is time for Day of the Dead.

This boy is cleaning a grave. People help clean and decorate the graves of those who do not have any living family or friends.

Dia de los Muertos

When night falls on November 1, people return to the graveyard to spend the entire night. Some Mexican families and neighbors form a long **procession** to the graveyard, carrying arches and crosses. Outside the cemetery, vendors may set up ice cream and food stands. Inside the cemetery, families set out their feast. Incense and candles are lit.

A woman lays out a feast for the spirit of her dead brother on his grave.

Families spend the whole night in the graveyard on Day of the Dead. They eat, sing, talk, and play music together.

Families pray or sit quietly by the grave. Some people play guitars or listen to music on radios they bring. Fireworks are set off to light the path home for the dead. At dawn on November 2, the Bible is read or a mass is held. People say goodbye to the spirits of loved ones for another year.

Let's Dance

These children are dressed for a dance performance for a Day of the Dead fiesta. The boy is wearing the costume for *La Danza de los Viejitos*.

Each region of Mexico has its own way of celebrating Day of the Dead. In some places, people perform dances during parties called *fiestas* as an important part of the celebration.

In Michoacán, a Mexican state, a dance called *La Danza de los Viejitos* takes place. *La Danza de los Viejitos* means "Dance of the Old Men." Boys and men dress up like old men. They walk with their bodies bent over. They dance slowly. As the music speeds up, the dancers move faster, as if the old men were young again. Near the end, the dancers move slowly as if old men again. In Aztec times, this dance was performed to honor a god called Huehueteotl who was always shown as an old man.

Skull masks are worn by some people to scare away the spirits who are reluctant to leave the world of the living on November 2.

29

Americans Celebrate

Day of the Dead is also celebrated outside of Mexico, by people of Mexican heritage. Many Mexican people live in the United States in Texas, California, and other states. Those Mexican Americans also celebrate Day of the Dead to honor their heritage, and to remember the spirits of the dead.

Mexican Americans celebrate Day of the Dead with altars, daytime processions to the graveyard, and all the special treats of the Mexican celebration. In some cities, there are also parades and *fiestas*. Some communities also have Native Mexican drummers and dancers to entertain people who take part in the celebrations.

30

A girl performs in a parade wearing a traditional Aztec costume in a Day of the Dead celebration in California, U.S.A.

Glossary

afterlife The belief that there is another life after this one

ancestor Someone from whom one is descended; a relative from way back

deceased Dead

depart To leave

descendant The children, grandchildren, great-grandchildren, and so on, of someone

empire A kingdom or country that rules over many other areas

folk music The traditional music of the people of a certain place

procession Parade

Roman Catholic Church A branch of Christianity headed by the Pope

symbol An image, word, or object that stands for something else

underworld A spirit world that is usually thought to be below the Earth

Index

Printed in the U.S.A.